CULTURE BY DESIGN
The new rules for employee
driven corporate culture

CULTURE BY DESIGN
The new rules for employee driven corporate culture

Ian Adkins

FUTURES BY DESIGN

2017

First published in Great Britain 2017

By Futures by Design Ltd

www.FuturesByDesign.com

First Printing: 2017

ISBN 978-0-244-30795-0

To Becca, Tasha and Charlie — my support, my inspiration and my wisest critic

Contents

Ian Adkins

Acknowledgements

A special thank you to everyone who has made this book possible, especially to my mentors throughout my professional journey who have shaped my thinking, approach and development.

In my military career a huge debt is owed to Lord Richard Dannatt, Lieutenant General Andrew Figgures, Major General Tim Tyler, Major General Mitch Mitchell, Brigadier Ian Simpson, Brigadier Peter Sharpe, and Brigadier Bill O'Leary.

My intellectual and professional development has been hugely varied and therefore I must thank a diverse array of hugely talented people especially Professor John Powell, Dr Sian Watt, Dr Leandro Herrero, Richard Bentley, Chris Samsa, Dr Andrew Murrison, Chris Howard, Johnnie Cass and Shellie Hunt for all believing in me, pushing me to achieve more and inspiring me to be more.

There are also numerous colleagues, clients and friends who have provided so much help, support, guidance and friendship. I must make mention of the following: Andrew Carwardine, Phil Redman, Kieron White, Nigel Hall, Neil Watkins, Max Joy, Deborah Jones, Wale Buraimoh, Rachel Bamber, Sarah Short, Gilbert Kearns, Rob Scott and Kevin Yong. There is also Mike Smith who has helped to steer my business thinking in recent times. I am indebted to you all in so many different ways and to many other former clients and colleagues, too many to mention, from whom I have learnt so much.

Finally, a mention to Lesley for encouraging me to finish this book and for keeping me on track. Thank you.

Ian Adkins

Preface

This book has been written as a practitioner's guide to help you as a business leader, change manager, internal communicator, HR professional or consultant to see a different and, I think, better way to design and deliver corporate culture change. I too am a practitioner of change and not a researcher or academic. I have seen a series of ideas that really seem to work, especially in combination, and want to share these insights with a community of liked minded people.

Nothing in this book is radically new or revolutionary on its own however as a combination is still uncommon, especially in larger, more traditional organizations. Every element exists out there in the public domain and I have attempted to reference those sources for you. What this book is designed to be is a combination of ideas and approaches that when used together create a powerful and innovative way of engaging people from across an organization to design and deliver corporate culture change whether that is a wholesale change of direction or a more focused change of behaviours in support of a new system, way of working or performance improvement.

Don't be fooled though. This is not an easy road nor a super-fast way of executing change. We are talking about people, but the approach described here works and creates lasting results. It is also about control: about who leads this change.

It is about taking back control from the big consultancies and training companies, that 'do' change 'to' organizations. It is about allowing employees to create change in a natural, organic, internally-led manner and one that creates energy, activism and a sense of ownership. Fundamentally it is about an approach that really works unlike 80% of culture change initiatives.

This book is also designed, like the rules that it sets out, to serve as a catalyst for action and debate. My fervent hope is that a global community of business leaders and change practitioners will gather around this approach and will help to contribute to making this book fuller and more comprehensive as well as more useful in future editions. Hopefully we can form our own community of activist-practitioners who are looking for a different, and better, way of leading people-change.

If anything in this book strikes a chord, then do please join the mailing list and get in touch either through the website or direct through email or Twitter. Together, let's begin to transform culture change, one conversation at a time.

Ian Adkins
ian@futuresbydesign.com
@IanAdkins
Chalfont St Giles, May 2017

Introduction

Foundations for leading change

I am sure that you can remember your first day at work in your first job after school or university. Most of us were wide eyed, a little anxious and desperately keen to make a good impression. It was probably a somewhat daunting experience.

A little over 30 years ago I arrived at the Royal Military Academy Sandhurst, the home of officer training for the British Army, having graduated from university a few months earlier. I had looked forward to that day with excitement and trepidation for a long time. The first day was an extended series of dull administrative sessions: form filling, briefings and medical and dental inspections.

Day 2 was altogether different. It started with our first drill session taken by our platoon colour sergeant. He was very loud and, for reasons I did not understand at the time, he seemed very angry. He shouted at us and our shambolic attempts to march. A few hours later, we were laden with bags of new kit having been to the quartermaster's stores and were trying to march the mile or so back to our accommodation carrying it all. My arms ached, my hands burned from the hard, new straps on my kitbags, and my brain tried to make sense of this sudden shock to the system. I, and my new colleagues, just got on with it though. That afternoon, we met our new platoon commander, a soft spoken, pleasant officer with a ready smile and an assured professional air about him. He was what we all aspired to be and found ourselves watching him and learning much from him.

What we also noticed was how close our platoon commander and platoon sergeant were and the mutual respect that they had for each other. Even though one was a well-educated and socially polished officer and the other a hardened, tough NCO and veteran of the Falklands War.

That evening we were given tasks for getting some kit ready for the following day and were left to it. We rallied around and helped each other, especially those of us with some previous military experience. Bonds were established quickly and leaders within our midst became obvious as they helped others and calmed nerves. They too became role models for those with less experience.

Your first few days in your first permanent job might be more or less deeply ingrained in your memory but think back to what you were learning. You probably had an induction or orientation period whether days, weeks or months long. You would have been told all about your organization's rules, procedures and policies. You would have had your job role explained and perhaps some training or preparation specific to that.

Ian Adkins

So much of what you learned though was not written down in a manual or policy booklet. You picked it up from what the people around you said and did. A common example of what is not written down but which forms an integral part of the working day is what you do for lunch. Do you bring sandwiches, go to the staff canteen, or the café over the road? Do you eat with colleagues or on your own? Typically, we look around us, watch what others do and follow their lead. If there are several patterns of behaviour then we look to someone a bit like us but more experienced, or to our new team leader, and simply do what they do.

When you started that that new job what you were doing in those first few days was absorbing the prevailing corporate culture. You learnt quickly and much of what you learnt about how to act, how to work and how to interact with colleagues was simply picked up by observation and copying. You kept your eyes and ears open and followed the lead of others, as I did at Sandhurst.

In the British Army, the relationship between a junior officer and his platoon sergeant is one of the most complex but also (when it works well) one of the most incredibly powerful leadership relationships. The young officer is in charge of the platoon by rank and by appointment, but his or her deputy is someone with 5, 10 or more years' extra professional as well as life experience. The junior officer is well advised to listen and learn whilst also trying to appear authoritative, confident and in control. This is a complex professional and personal relationship and one that cannot be learnt purely from a book or in a classroom. Observing it in action is key and emulating successful examples is vital. Indeed, so much of what we do throughout our professional lives is absorbed like this.

The realities of organizational change

Given this grounding that we all have in observing our colleagues' behaviours, imitating them and learning from those closest to us, then it is amazing that we seem to adopt very different approaches as we become more senior and begin to lead organizational change ourselves.

In my military career, both regular and reserve, I worked my way up to leading a battalion of over 300 people and have held several staff jobs, four of them at Ministry of Defence or Army HQ level. There I saw many corporate change initiatives and as a consultant over many years I have been part of numerous change programmes. They have varied in nature from process changes, technology change, strategy development, strategic planning and in more recent years to culture change. What has struck me is how focused we all become on structures, procedures and processes and how confident we are that these will deliver tangible and meaningful change. Especially when led or organized by us.

Yet time and again, that 3 or 6-month change project that was going to revolutionize how we worked and the environment in which we worked, extends out to 12 or 24 months and results seem slow to materialize. When we look at what is happening around us, we realize with horror and resignation that not a lot has really changed. People are working and interacting in more or less the same way; the place still has a similar feel; and things are perhaps only marginally better than they were 2 years previously. Has that happened to you? Have you see this?

I worked for one large corporate client some years ago on a safety culture project. They had dozens of similar projects running concurrently, all over the place. They were utterly fixated on reorganising themselves; creating new forms; new procedures; new job roles; and communication campaigns that used ever more elaborate emails, glossier and better produced magazines and posters, video campaigns, and even touring actors simulating common risk scenarios. I got involved both at the strategic end and then later at the operational end with front-line leaders.

I really felt sorry for those guys. They were inundated with safety talks, training courses, management briefings, executive visits and then workshops with consultants like me. I tried hard to make my two days with them as experiential and meaningful as I could but it was hopeless really. I felt demoralised and began to search for a better way to deliver corporate culture change that both delivered on the executive level aspiration whether that was safety, customer centricity, agility or innovation but also crucially, something that actually gave front line staff something tangible that they could *do* differently. Appealing to them logically and emotionally can be quite successful in getting people to buy-in to a new approach, but if they still don't have the concrete behaviours or actions to take, little or nothing will really change on a day to day level.

The people I met on that project had heard it all before. I know because they told me! They were hard-pressed people who didn't need to hear the messages again but just in a different format. They wanted to know the answer to the question: "what can I *do* differently in my job tomorrow to make this all work?". They didn't need fluffy words and feelings. They wanted something tangible, practical and actionable. Something they could understand and take away. Something they felt comfortable to do themselves. Their words to me were direct, forthright and hard-hitting. They made a real impact on me.

A manifesto for change

So, began my journey and what follows is the results of what I have discovered over many years from reading, courses that I have attended, results from client work as well as working at the feet of masters in the field and talking to lots of other practitioners too. I reiterate that every element is out there somewhere, and used in combination by some, but in my experience, is little understood nor used in large scale corporate change projects.

You may ask why this is. In part, it is probably down to some of my colleagues in the large consultancies or training houses which have a vested interest in selling large scale consultant- or trainer-led solutions. However, as we have seen simply 'sheep-dipping' everyone through an engagement workshop or extensive communications campaign, whilst appealing in its simplicity, does not generally work. Nothing much really changes. We are all so busy it is always easy to call in the outside experts to 'do' change to us. But it doesn't deliver long term sustainable behavioural change by and large.

So, what follows is not a quick cure but is something that can produce deep, lasting and sustainable results with changes observable within months. It needs to be structured and staffed with the right people, probably with a bit of outside expert help, but above all it relies on the sort of insights outlined in the first couple of pages of this chapter. It is also informed by recent research results from an array of fields including cognitive psychology, neuroscience, behavioural economics and political science amongst others.

Introducing the new rules

So, let me outline the 5 new rules for creating a Culture by Design that will deliver real and lasting change before expanding in greater detail in subsequent chapters.

I use the term TransACT™ to summarise the 5 rules. TransACT™ is short for Transformational Activism and is shown graphically in Figure 1. TransACT™ seeks not just a transformation in the organization but in all of the participants and activists, involved too.

In short, TransACT™ creates behavioural transformation for an organization by using a carefully defined set of granular behaviours (Rule 1 - ACTIONS FIRST) which are spread around the organization using an infection model. The behaviours must be defined against a clear organizational objective but also be articulated in a way that galvanises people into action around an aspirational goal (Rule 2 – AIM HIGHER). This will be achieved by using peer selected change champions who are trained in activist techniques and then organized into a cohesive social movement (Rule 3 - ACTIVISM DELIVERS). That movement will spread the behaviours through the informal organization that functions alongside the visible, formal organization of every corporation. The best connected and most influential people, wherever they sit in the organization will be best able to achieve this as they are the authentic leaders (Rule 4 – AUTHENTICITY LEADS).

TransACT Rules

ACTIONS FIRST
Work to change people's behaviours using behaviourist tools knowing that hearts and minds will follow.

AIM HIGHER
Be clear about why you are embarking on this change and articulate it as a cause worth fighting for.

AUTHENTICITY LEADS
Understand that the informal organisation and its dynamics and work with it as much as the formal organisation.

ACTIVISM DELIVERS
Combine the cause, informal organisation and behaviourist tools to create change using a social movement.

AUTONOMY WINS
The activists of the social movement need to be trusted, empowered and free to operate if they are to succeed.

Figure 1. The TransACT rules.

The whole process will need to be carefully planned and directed by a campaign team who recruit, prepare and organize the activists or champions and orchestrate the spread of the behaviours and, crucially, the growth of the social movement. This will only happen effectively and sustainably, if the movement and its leaders are given full autonomy by the organization's executive leadership team. This requires a leap of faith in some organizations and senior leaders will need to step back and adopt a supportive and enabling style of leadership that allows a wildfire of new behaviours to be ignited and then spread throughout the organization. If they can do this then the results both in terms of project aims and wider personal development and employee empowerment will pay huge dividends downstream (Rule 5 – AUTONOMY WINS).

Emerging best practice in the field of social activism suggests that a successful and vibrant movement does more than just mobilise its people around transactional objectives; it invests in the leaders of the movement at all levels, increasing not just its capacity as a movement but that of the people involved too.

In this way, TransACT™ seeks to go beyond traditional change management approaches. Not only does it address the problem of low success rates in linear, top-down change management approaches but also seeks to make the whole process something of broader and longer term value. TransACT™ aims to be transformative not just for organizations but also for everyone involved too.

Ian Adkins

Chapter 1: The Problem of Change

Traditional change management

The evidence suggests that traditional change management does not work. Indeed, the failure rates seen would, quite simply, not be accepted in any other area of business.

The 'statistic' that some 70% of organizational change projects fail is quoted frequently. The source of this figure was survey data and out-of-context remarks by Professors Kotter and Nohria of Harvard University[1]. It turns out that overall, 70% might be an exaggeration but only a modest one. Dozens of surveys put the actual failure rate at around 50%, for example[2]:

▶ 50% of mergers (totalling one trillion dollars in the United States alone) fail to deliver value[3].

▶ 17% of large IT projects go so badly that they can threaten the very existence of the company, and large IT projects run an average of 45% over

---

[1] Hughes, M. (2011, Dec 6). *Do 70 per cent of all organizational change initiatives really fail?* Journal of Change Management, 11(4), 451 – 464.
[2] Gibbons, P. (2015). *The Science of Successful Organizational Change, how leaders set strategy, change behaviour, and create an agile culture.* USA: Pearson Education.
[3] Bain US and European Acquisition Success Study (2007).

budget, while delivering 56% less value than predicted[4].

► 41% of change projects were described as successful in an IBM report[5].

Beyond the headline figure, it seems that failure also varies significantly according to the type of change that is being attempted. In one study by UK researcher Dr Martin Smith, in which he summarized 49 separate case studies, there was considerable variation in the success and failure rates. Whilst the sample size was relatively small, the overall failure rate was just below 50% which echoed the studies above. What was most telling though was the range in the success rates observed from strategy deployment (58%), restructuring (46%) and technology change (40%) at the most successful end of the spectrum through to software development/installation (26%), business expansion (20%) and culture change (19%).

It comes as little surprise that in this survey less than 1 in 5 culture change projects achieved a successful outcome as this seems to be the empirical evidence that

---

[4] Bloch, M., Blumberg, S., & Laartz, J. (2012, October). Delivering large scale IT projects on time, on budget, and on value. *McKinsey Quarterly* (online).

[5] Jorgenson, H., Owen, L., & Neus, A. (2013). *Making change work*. IBM Future of Enterprise.

most business leaders have acquired from their own experience of cultural change projects over the years in their own careers. Perhaps you have too?

Imagine if we had an 80% failure rate in new IT system deployments, product launches or recruitment procedures. Businesses would fail and those responsible would be held to account, and most likely be fired. When it comes to people-change the high failure rate seems to be accepted, even expected, yet the prevailing tools of change management keep getting employed over and over: a classic case of doing the same thing again and again, but expecting different results.

Cultural change management

Why is cultural change so hard? It seems to stem from our own personal ideas and experiences of what 'change' is and significantly on the prevailing models and methodologies that are taught at business schools and employed by *'change managers'*.

There is a plethora of approaches to managing organization change, often reduced to a series of steps or stages: Kotter's 8 steps, Booz & Co.'s ten principles or Prosci's 5 building blocks; there are also a wide range of popular ideas on how to effect change as well as the widely varying individual ideas and approaches of the leaders who are overseeing change based on their own past experiences, training and education. The problem is that each of these is based on a particular theory or understanding of human nature and how people change. The evidence suggests many are not particularly effective or may actually be highly counterproductive, as Paul Gibbons[6] observes:

▶ Traditional methods of stakeholder communication during change focus on providing information. However, when faced with ideological resistance, research suggests that providing more facts may induce more resistance, not lessen it.

▶ Most models of personal change focus on changing attitudes first in order to change behaviours, i.e. "think your way into a new way of acting". Research suggests that, just as often, people "act their way into a new way of thinking".

The fundamental problem is that business leaders tend to place great reliance on their own understanding of human behaviour based on their own personal experiences in life and in business, especially in their formative years. Whilst these personal insights from experience may be more or less valid at the individual level, they tend not to be particularly helpful in understanding the complexity of achieving change in the large, dynamic systems that are modern corporations.

---

[6] Gibbons, P. (2015). *The Science of Successful Organizational Change, how leaders set strategy, change behaviour, and create an agile culture.* USA: Pearson Education.

Ian Adkins

The picture gets harder when leaders are bombarded by an array of approaches and ideas, often popularized by the writing or inspirational talks of gurus; some of whom are researchers and real experts in their fields, however far more have little if any evidence to underpin their assertions on the best approach to follow. Paul Gibbons offers a harsh critique of many of these ideas and gurus in his book *The Science of Successful Organizational Change*. Indeed, he paints a particularly grim picture of management education as well as most established ways for managing change. He even suggests "we should euthanize change management" but accepts that this is neither desirable nor possible in reality. What is required, he says, is a more rigorous, evidence-based approach to managing change.

An alternative approach

It is this challenge that was the catalyst for the development of TransACT™ and the idea of creating a community of like-minded change leaders and practitioners to refine it further. It is an attempt to offer a practical, evidence-based approach for cultural change in organizations and draws together a wide range of robust and proven insights and approaches in to one cohesive and powerful framework.

The rest of this book will unpack the methodology as it stands and outline how to employ it. This is a first attempt and is a personal synthesis of ideas, evidence and experience gained over 30 years and is offered as a start point. I urge you to read the remainder of this book critically but kindly noting down your own reactions and thoughts: do please share these with me.

Ian Adkins

Chapter 2: TransACT™ Overview

A multi-disciplinary Framework

TransACT™ deliberately and quite explicitly draws on a wide range of influences to create an effective and powerful approach to creating cultural change in organizations from small enterprises right through to globally dispersed, multi-nationals. It is designed as a collection of best practices. Indeed, the essential ingredients are well published and generally accepted, however some are not yet widely established, mainstream approaches. In combination, they are still unusual but not entirely unique. The key influences are highlighted in detail in the next section but in broad terms they are built on the areas of scientific endeavour that Paul Gibbons[7] identifies as offering the most promise for the future evolution of organizational change:

▶ Focus on human flourishing
▶ Neuroscience
▶ Neobehaviourism
▶ Integration with other disciplines

---

[7] Gibbons, P. (2015). *The Science of Successful Organizational Change, how leaders set strategy, change behaviour, and create an agile culture.* USA: Pearson Education.

Focus on human flourishing

Movements such as "positive psychology" are a move away from the psychology of mental illness and dysfunction, and towards the promotion of human flourishing. The best ideas on flourishing combine happiness with engagement, meaning and contribution (service), making flourishing a more robust concept than happiness and one that we can usefully draft into the world of business change and use as a general theme in TransACT™.

Neuroscience

The relatively new field of neuroscience gives us an insight into the biology behind human behaviour. Whilst hyped up by some and not really at a stage where it can deliver robust tools, it is an area of great promise. One of the problems is that the field, especially the prefix "neuro" is overused and has been misappropriated especially for models that are more realistically based on cognitive psychology, such as the 'Neuro-leadership' field espoused by David Rock. He has nevertheless produced some highly useful and grounded models which are referenced later; their root though is mostly in cognitive psychology not in neuroscience. Regardless, we can draw upon the rich seams of golden nuggets that run through these interconnected fields.

Ian Adkins

Neobehaviourism

A new focus on human behaviours and how to close the gap between thought and action provides a wealth of tools and insights for effective organizational as well as even societal change. The term though needs careful definition in our context: it is dogged by a traditional carrot and stick, rewards and sanctions, understanding of behaviourism that runs deep in most leaders' understanding of human change. Furthermore, as a title it runs up against some political science theory which can generate some unnecessary misunderstandings. So, long as we interpret neo-behaviourism as the latest thinking from research into human behaviours that suggests that changing behaviours first can be as successful, if not more so, than changing thinking and beliefs then this term can work well for us.

Integration with other disciplines

The complexity of applied business psychology when it comes to change in large organizations means that there are significant contributions that can be made from the new knowledge coming out of a vast range of other disciplines: law, public policy, public health, medicine, economics, religion, anthropology, philosophy, neurobiology, systems theory and even political campaigning. Some of these are evident in the next section and others will offer great opportunities for the future evolution of TransACT™.

TransACT™ principles

TransACT™ is built upon a logical framework of five principles. Whilst each can be summarised succinctly, most are in reality a blend of ideas, tools and insights. In the chapters that follow the breadth of inputs is highlighted as well as the key influences. These principles are presented as rules: not to be followed slavishly but as empirical guides as to what fundamentally works when it comes to large scale organizational culture change. There are broad indications as to how these would be implemented but this book is about setting out the breadth of the stall that is TransACT™ and to stimulate debate amongst practitioners and those that want to bring this approach into their organizations.

Chapter 3: Rule 1 – Aim Higher

Start with Why?

TransACT™ starts with the idea that to create a fundamental shift in an organization then you need to generate significant energy, focus and determination to underpin this endeavour and to give it the momentum it needs to build sustainable change across an organization. Indeed, I suggest it should be expressed with the passion and commitment of a 'cause'; a cause that everyone involved can believe in and become passionate about. If this is achieved, then everything else follows smoothly. The greatest curse in cultural change is to have a vague goal expressed in uninspiring, managerialist terms; if it doesn't arouse some emotion then the rest becomes ultimately so much harder.

A great place to start with developing a motivational cause is to follow Simon Sinek's advice contained in his book[8] *Start with Why* as well his popular TED Talk[9]. He has a powerful model for inspirational leadership which he puts across with simplicity and real power. His model is based on a "a golden circle" and at its centre is the single question "Why?". He argues that neuroscience tells us that our brain's decision making operates

---

[8] Sinek, S. (2011). *Start with why: How great leaders inspire everyone to take action.* New York: Portfolio / Penguin.

[9] http://www.ted.com/talks/simon_sinek_how_great_leaders_inspire_action.html.

rapidly and unconsciously, and much of it happens at an emotional level – whether we like that idea or not. If we are moved by "why" someone does what they do, then we are far more likely to follow them and, in turn, they are more likely to be successful.

He uses the examples of Apple, Martin Luther King and the Wright brothers. The point that sums it up best is perhaps that Martin Luther King Jr "gave the *I have a dream'* speech, not the *I have a plan'* speech." He moved people at a deep level with his powerful oratory and his raw emotion. Whilst an organizational culture change initiative is unlikely to reach these heights it is nevertheless necessary to go beyond the bland and get clear on the 'why' and ensure that it is expressed as a positive, inspirational cause that people will want to get behind.

I have seen all sorts of examples in my consulting work. Too often the underlying theme is one of efficiency, compliance, quality, agility, being customer centric or just being safer. However, none of these as terms raises passions and all are generic.

Once, I had to stand and give a long series of internal presentations to client groups about a new way of working which focused on how to file documents in a new system. The focus on filing and compliance with legal requirements was worthy and factually correct but made the whole thing, sound really rather dull. Whereas in reality it was fundamentally about unleashing the power of shared information in the organization and how this could dramatically improve both the efficiency of the way people worked but also the quality of what they produced. A dynamic theme - a reason 'why' - based on that would have helped engage people far more easily. In the end that project was a great success but it was perhaps harder work than necessary.

A good example from a safety context is the UK rail infrastructure provider Network Rail's focus on 'Everyone home safe every day". Using this sort of language moves staff away from compliance and vague long term aspirations to a daily goal that everyone can focus on, each and every day. At the team level, it gets personal.

Power up your cause

Finding a reason why and expressing it in clear and powerful language can be difficult when the initial catalyst is a mundane compliance issue or need to replace an aging technology. However, there will always be aspirational hopes that come with the changes and it is important to spend the time and energy in connecting with these and clearly expressing the project's aim around them. It is also vital to find a form of words that convey these with clarity, meaning and purpose.

Time spent in this will pay dividends later given the duration and complexity that is likely to follow. Building and then maintaining momentum around changes that might take a year or two, or even three, to deliver fully, is critical. People need something that will evoke commitment, energy and passion to take them through the long months of making change a reality. Let them *'power up'* their organization through their people, put their values *'into action'* or make their brand *'live every day'* within the organization as well as outside.

Should the solution not come to mind quickly then spend time talking to employees, perhaps in focus groups, to find out what they would really like to change themselves and how they would like to refer to it. Find the touchpoints and the sources of energy and weave those in to your cause.

In the enthusiasm to get going this step is easily lost as people dive into the project's details but if the top team hasn't defined it then the project team need to have this as one of their first tasks before looking at the fundamental nature of the changes that they will make happen.

Chapter 4: Rule 2 – Actions First

Think behaviours

The most fundamental tenet of TransACT™ is that changing behaviours is at the heart of changing a culture and comes before anything else. Organizational culture is often described as 'what people do when no one is looking'. In other words, it is the day to day reality of how people act and interact in the workplace ignoring all of the rules, procedures, processes, value statements and press releases. It is the little things that people say and do; it is how they naturally behave at work. It's what you would see if you were the proverbial fly-on-the-wall.

This is completely different to most prevailing change methodologies which stress a hearts and minds approach. The problem with that is however strongly someone buys into the logic of the new customer initiative or safety campaign, they will continue to act in a particular way out of habit and of social convention: if everyone around you is behaving in a certain way, then why should you stand out and be different?

There are entire fields of study based on these ideas: traditional psychologists and behaviourists have made way for neobehaviourists, and behavioural economics has become mainstream in helping governments and corporations to understand and use psychological, social, cognitive, and emotional factors on the economic decisions of individuals and institutions and the consequences of these. For simplicity, we will group the insights that are of most utility to our endeavours under the heading of neobehaviourism.

Neobehaviourism

Neobehaviourism can be defined[10] as the 21st Century school of applied research that emphasizes changing behaviours without first changing hearts and minds. In his book *The Science of Successful Organizational Change*, Paul Gibbons identifies the following positive features of neobehaviourist approaches:

▶ We can measure behaviours accurately, and hence can assess cause and effect scientifically, and know whether policies or interventions really work.

▶ We can care what people think and feel, sincerely, and not just so they do what we want them to do.

▶ Behaviour never lies. Phenomena such as engagement and commitment can be defined in behavioural terms, not just be self-report surveys – that is, by what people actually *do*, rather than what they think or feel.

▶ Some neobehaviourist methods are well studied, and so provide evidence-based guidance for managers.

---

[10] Gibbons, P. (2015). The Science of Successful Organizational Change, how leaders set strategy, change behaviour, and create an agile culture. USA: Pearson Education.

Ian Adkins

▶ The methods produce real-world change, and not just change inside people's heads.

The underpinning mantra is *'you can act your way into a new way of thinking, rather than think your way into a new way of acting'*. He goes on to identify four promising areas of neobehaviourist practices that are beginning to infiltrate business:

▶ **Behavioural specificity.** Behavioural change can only really occur if the behaviours are specified in detailed behavioural terms. This definition must have clear and unambiguous meaning to both the person displaying the behaviour and anyone observing it and it needs to be repeatable by anyone across the spectrum of environments and situations experienced in the organization. In this way people know exactly what they need to do and can clearly see the new behaviours being displayed by others.

▶ **Choice architecture.** Choice architecture was made famous by the book *Nudge*[11] by Richard Thaler and Cass Sunstein. The key idea in the book is that individuals retain full autonomy over their decisions in a particular situation but attempts are made to shape their choice, or to nudge them in a particular direction. This is a hot topic for public

---

[11] Thaler, R. H., Sunstein, C. R., & Soundview Executive Book Summaries. (2010). Nudge: Improving decisions about health, wealth, and happiness. Concordville, Pa.: Soundview Executive Book Summaries.

policy makers and areas such as marketing. Examples include supermarkets putting staple goods such as bread and milk at the back of a store so you must walk past impulse buys and special promotions; or the opt-out rather than opt-in systems for organ donation (99% of Austrians are registered organ donors compared to 43% in the US, for example). Nudge tactics can also be used to reduce choices down to a small number, say a bronze, silver and gold option. Too many choices confuse people, raise doubts and ultimately defer or even prevent buying decisions being made.

► **Mastery of habits.** Much has been written about how most human functioning on a day to day basis is made up of habits and rituals that become ingrained and which dominate most of our daily actions. In the same way business culture can be seen as a collection of habits, routines and rituals performed more or less unconsciously because that is "how we do things here". Changing culture can be seen as a collective changing of those habits. This insight combined with the knowledge of individual habit change, behavioural specificity and choice architecture can be combined into the core of a highly effective behavioural and cultural change programme.

Ian Adkins

The emerging neobehaviourist research and best practices have been adopted by the UK Cabinet Office's Behavioural Insights Team[12] who have combined these with Professor Robert Cialdini's insights on influence, summarized in his classic book *Influence: The Psychology of Persuasion*[13]. The resulting framework is called MINDSPACE and is shown in Figure 2 below. The

Messenger	we are heavily influenced by who communicates information
Incentives	our responses to incentives are shaped by predictable mental shortcuts such as strongly avoiding losses
Norms	we are strongly influenced by what others do
Defaults	we 'go with the flow' of pre-set options
Salience	our attention is drawn to what is novel and seems relevant to us
Priming	our acts are often influenced by sub-conscious cues
Affect	our emotional associations can powerfully shape our actions
Commitments	we seek to be consistent with our public promises, and reciprocate acts
Ego	we act in ways that make us feel better about ourselves

Figure 2. UK government MINDSPACE framework.

constituent elements are based on considerable research and have been field-tested and shown great promise; the framework is used to help UK government

[12] Dolan, P., Hallsworth, M., Halpern, D., King, D., & Vlaev, I. (2009). *Mindspace: Influencing behaviour through public policy. Institute for Government (UK).* Retrieved from https://www.instituteforgovernment.org.uk/sites/default/files/publications/MINDSPACE.pdf.
[13] Cialdini, R. B. (2011). *Influence: The psychology of persuasion.* New York, NY: Collins.

policy makers and serves as a robust framework to use in TransACT™ interventions.

Employing behaviourist insights

There are a series of insights from this field of neo-behaviourism that we can use in our work to change corporate cultures but there are two key insights above all.

Firstly, that we must focus relentlessly on identifying a small number of key behaviours that are tangible, repeatable, observable and measurable. Jon Katzenbach, one of the foremost applied thinkers and practitioners in this field, and his colleagues in the Katzenbach Centre, call them the "critical few" behaviours[14]. They describe them as keystone behaviours which are the patterns of acting which can shape an entire organization's culture.

Successfully identifying just a small number of behaviours and then describing them with the specificity required can be a challenge, both practical and political; it as much art as science in getting to the heart of the matter and to encapsulating the specific behaviours in the right way. Once done however, these few behaviours become the core around which the rest of your culture change initiative is built and once connected to

---

[14] Hull, K. (2017). *Getting to the Critical Few Behaviours That Can Drive Cultural Change.* Retrieved from https://www.strategy-business.com/blog/Getting-to-the-Critical-Few-Behaviors-That-Can-Drive-Cultural-Change

your cause becomes a powerful catalyst to bring about meaningful change.

The second key insight is the importance of the 'messenger' for communicating new behaviours to others (as identified in MINDSPACE) and how this is closely linked to norming. That is how we are strongly influenced by what others do and tend to conform to the behavioural norm set by the people around us. In short, if the keystone behaviours can be demonstrated and communicated by genuinely influential people across the organization then it is much more likely to spread naturally and quickly. This leads us into the next rule in TransACT™ which is centred around finding and engaging those influential people to help in spreading new behaviours.

Culture by Design

Chapter 5: Rule 3 – Authenticity Leads

Working in the informal organization

In putting the MINDSPACE framework into practice as a tool for culture change, we can do no better than to look at the extensive work of Jon Katzenbach on the informal world that exists in every organization. He identified[15] the fundamental divide that exists between the formal, structured organization that we see, learn about in business education and operate in day-to-day and the informal organization of social networks and ad hoc communities that occur naturally. Critically he said that leaders need to embrace both and learn the complementary skills of *managing* in the formal organization and *mobilizing* in the informal one.

He explored the idea of creating cultural change through the informal organization in his paper[16], the *10 Principles of Organizational Culture*, in which he identifies a novel framework for culture change based on neo-behaviourist insights. He reinforces the idea that "behaviours are the most powerful determinant of real

---

[15] Katzenbach, R., & Khan, Z. (2010). *Leading outside the lines*. San Francisco, CA; A Wiley.

[16] Katzenbach, R. (2016). *10 principles of organizational culture*. Retrieved from https://www.strategy-business.com/media/file/sb82_10_Principles_of_Organizational_Culture.pdf.

change. What people actually do matters more than what they say or believe." In his formula, there are 4 particularly important principles which stand out and have been absorbed into the TransACT™ framework. They build on the insights in the previous chapters and make them actionable:

▶ **Focus on a critical few behaviours.** These behaviours should be tangible, actionable, repeatable, observable and measurable. In developing them organizations should be highly selective, picking just the "critical few" that have the greatest impact when put into practice by a significant number of people. To do this, they must be codified: that is translated into simple, practical actions that people can take every day and which, when installed in a group of influential people, can be spread by imitation across the organization.

▶ **Deploy the authentic informal leaders.** Authentic informal leaders are found in every organization but are not always recognized as such, indeed they may not be your "star performers"[17]; they can be overlooked and under-used, especially in something like culture change. They can be identified through interviews, surveys and tools

---

[17] Carpenter, R. (2016). *How to Find and Engage Authentic Informal Leaders.* Retrieved from https://www.strategy-business.com/blog/How-to-Find-and-Engage-Authentic-Informal-Leaders.

such as organizational network analysis[18], which enable maps of complex internal social relations to be created. These leaders can be powerful allies in influencing the behaviour of those around them.

▶ **Use cross-organizational methods to go viral.** Katzenbach says in his article *10 principles of organizational culture* that *"ideas can spread virally across organizational departments and functions, as well as from the bottom up."* It is suggested that social media (blogs, Facebook, LinkedIn, Twitter and the like) can be used, not by senior leaders, but by the authentic, informal leaders. This sort of spread of information can be more effective than traditional methods and when it comes to critical behaviours, people are more likely to believe and adopt them if they see and hear from trusted sources that this is "the way we do things around here" now. This credible social proof is far more compelling than carefully crafted testimonials coming down from the central communications department.

▶ **Align programmatic efforts with behaviours.** Finally, he highlights the fact that it is also important to align traditional ways of doing business across the organization with the new behaviours and associated implementation activities. Fundamentally the informality of this approach to culture

---

[18] Laseter, T. and Cross, R. (2006). *The Craft of Connection.* Retrieved from: https://www.strategy-business.com/article/06302.

change must match with all of the components of the formal organization.

Turning informal leaders into activists

Katzenbach's principles have been extended as an approach to organizational behavioural change by Leandro Herrero who has written two books[19],[20] on a culture change methodology called Viral Change™ which he describes as "the art of social infection". There is much crossover with Katzenbach but Herrero introduces the additional idea of turning authentic, informal leaders into activists within the informal organization, what he calls World 2, and forming them into a social movement. Indeed, his blog has a series of references[21] to the utility of using social movements in cultural change and the need to learn from political and social movements. This seems to be a key extension to his earlier work and that of Jon Katzenbach, and lays the foundation for the fourth TransACT™ principle: that we can turbocharge cultural change by using activists as part of a social movement.

---

[19] Herrero, L. (2008). *Viral Change™: the alternative to slow, painful and unsuccessful management of change in organizations*. UK: Meeting Minds.

[20] Herrero, L. (2011). *Homo Imitans, the art of social infection: Viral Change™ in action*. UK: Meeting Minds.

[21] A good example is this: https://leandroherrero.com/business-discovers-the-social-movement-language-i-hope-we-dont-corporatize-it/. The main blog is at: https://leandroherrero.com/.

Ian Adkins

Chapter 6: Rule 4 – Activism Delivers

Mobilizing vs organizing activists

There is much to learn from the world of political campaigning and civic action especially the research in recent years into particularly effective political parties and civic associations. The lessons from the Barack Obama campaigns of 2008 and 2012 have been widely reported and more recently so have the lessons of the Bernie Sanders campaign of 2016. Most focus on the political campaigning and aspects such as the highly targeted and effective use of social media not on the activist organization itself. Hahrie Han in his book[22] *How Organizations Develop Activists* reports on his research into the manner in which effective movements are organized and led. This provides key insights for mobilizing and organising a social movement within an organization, using the authentic, informal leaders identified by Katzenbach. Indeed, he establishes a clear framework for success in creating an activist movement with breadth and depth.

Han's fundamental conclusion was that "what really differentiates the highly active [volunteer] associations is the way they transform their members' motivations

[22] Han, H. (2014). *How organizations develop activists*. New York, NY: Oxford University Press.

and capacities for involvement". It was the "organizations that combined transformational organizing with transactional mobilizing [which] were able to achieve higher levels of activism over time." The distinction between *'transactional mobilizing'* and *'transformational organising'* is the central theme of his book. He draws a clear distinction between the movement leaders for each these, who he calls *mobilisers* and *organizers*.

Mobilising is essential to all of these organizations: it is the largely transactional business of recruiting new members, getting people to events and the mechanistic activism of completing templated letters and forwarding given messages, often through social media. Mobilisers understand that their activists have a sense of purpose and want to 'do something' but that they are also busy people, so their activism is divided in to small, discrete, straightforward tasks and distributed widely in the hope that enough people will take the requested action. The work of mobilizing tends to be centralized with a few people and focuses on generating transactional outcomes, such as a large number of participants at an event or many letters to an elected representative. Every social movement needs mobilisers; however, it tends to be the limit for the lower performing, less active associations studied by Han.

Organizers, by contrast, invest in developing the capacities of people to engage with others in activism and to become leaders. Mobilisers focus on maximizing the number of people involved without developing their capacity for action. Organising on the other hand has the potential to be transformational both in achieving the organization's aims but also for the people in the organization. Organizers cultivate their people, especially potential leaders so that they can not only recruit and mobilise others but also engage others in deeper, more impactful ways. This development of activist leadership potential creates a transformational experience which develops a self-interest in personal growth and deepens the sense of purpose as well as achievement of activists. This links well with the idea of human flourishing identified in Chapter 2 and suggests that this is a particularly important idea for us.

The power of a social movement

Han reports that the development of people's ability occurs on a little-and-often basis and encompasses training, coaching and reflection. Movements with a strong organising capability tend to be highly social, encouraging contact between members as well as giving them some strategic autonomy, showing them how their work fits in with the larger whole. These relational commitments become an important source of motivation. The commitment to activism is therefore borne not only out of commitment to the issue or cause, but also of commitment to other people. In these ways, it is not just people that power the movement: the movement also powers its people.

Culture by Design

In TransACT™, the formation and then growth of a social movement of activists is therefore key and is no minor undertaking. Indeed, it will represent the biggest single element of the project and require appropriate effort and resources, especially at the beginning whilst it is launching. Activists will need to be equipped with the keystone behaviours, recruited and trained as activists and given the tools as well as the permission to go forward and helped to create a vibrant and active social movement.

The initial preparation of the informal leaders and their transition into activists can usually be achieved in an intensive activist camp. Thereafter, local initiatives will need to be encouraged and supported, remembering that the organizing role, rather than mobilizing, is most fundamental for long term success. It is vital to invest in the people involved so as to increase their capacity to be capable activists within a coherent, dynamic movement. Creating the space and freedom for this to occur is a critical leadership challenge in this sort of undertaking. Leaders can have difficulty in letting go enough to do this but empowering your people will pay long term dividends in many ways, some of them quite unexpected.

Chapter 7: Rule 5 – Autonomy Wins

Understand motivation

Empowerment is a key theme in TransACT™ and we need to be clear on what this means at a human level. In particular, on what motivates and demotivates people. Neuroscience combined with cognitive psychology is helping us to create not just an understanding of human motivation and interaction but also generate frameworks that enable us to deploy these insights effectively in support of cultural change. David Rock has done much in this field to convert extensive research from a number of fields into a digestible and useful form. His book *Your Brain at Work*[23] is an easy read summarizing more extensive material published elsewhere. He includes a key model to support organizational culture change[24] called the SCARF model which has been adopted into TransACT™.

He suggests that our brains are constantly "on alert" for threats to guard against and furthermore that social needs are treated in the same way as basic needs, such

[23] Rock, D. (2009). *Your brain at work: Strategies for overcoming distraction, regaining focus, and working smarter all day long.* New York, NY: Harper Collins.

[24] Rock, D. (2012). Managing with the brain in mind. In *Don't blame your culture.* Booz & Company eBook retrieved from Amazon Kindle.

as safety, food and water. So, the brain handles every-day interactions with work colleagues, with the same power and intensity as it would have done tens of thousands of years ago when we had to fight hard to secure food, shelter and a mate and then to protect them. So, in a work environment people's brains are moving between two powerful emotional states: toward and away and we are easily put into an 'away' or threatened state by social threats every bit as powerfully as physical threats. Rock's model identifies five types of environmental stimuli that have a particular impact on whether we experience a toward emotion or away emotion.

► **Status**. Status to the brain is an extremely important resource. Your brain is constantly monitoring your status in any group. It literally assigns you a number in that group. When you feel like you're going up in status you start to feel some of the toward emotions. The brain sees a drop-in status as a threat to your life. This is as threatening to the brain as physical pain. Simply thinking about certain kinds of events, such as receiving feedback, speaking to someone that has a higher status than you in the company, or making a sales call, can give you a similar experience of status going down. Organizational change has huge scope for creating threats to people's status or perceived status.

► **Certainty**. Certainty is a fundamental driver of the brain. The brain is a prediction machine and prefers to go largely on automatic if it can. Any time we experience uncertainty we get a limbic system response. In other words, we experience more of the away emotions. A small amount of uncertainty can be pleasant. But when we get too much uncertainty the limbic system becomes aroused causing a powerful threat response.

▶ **Autonomy**. Autonomy is the experience of having choice. When someone feels that there is some choice in a given situation, then they're more likely to experience toward emotions. When you feel that you don't have any autonomy or choice then you may experience away emotions. Research has shown that in a stressful situation where people feel like they have choice they experience hardly any stress. The opposite is also true.

▶ **Relatedness**. Relatedness is about whether you consider a person a friend or foe. When you connect with people you like or can trust you get a decrease in the stress hormone cortisol and an injection of the feel-good hormone dopamine. In other words, you experience more toward emotions. When you meet someone that you don't trust you feel threatened. You start to feel more of the away emotions, an increase in cortisol and possibly adrenaline if the other person is considered a major threat.

▶ **Fairness**. Everyone likes to feel that they have been dealt with in a fair manner. When we feel that we have been treated unfairly, for example in a pay review, we experience away emotions, such as disappointment, anger, disillusionment and frustration. When we are treated fairly, for example receiving much more than we expected in a pay review, then we feel toward emotions, such as joy, happiness, motivation and commitment

The SCARF model can be interpreted and used for shaping individual one-to-one interactions in everyday business life as well as at an organizational level. Cultural change initiatives can easily create perceived threats in any one of the five SCARF dimensions. Conversely, using these insights positively can help to shape an initiative that is far more likely to succeed as it creates a positive, 'toward' motivation across all those impacted by the change. It is especially useful in helping the thinking of the main project team as well as the community of activists that are recruited to the cause.

Motivating the activist movement

The critical imperative for senior leaders is to use these SCARF dimensions to create a high-performing project team to run a TransACT™ project that is truly empowered to do so. This means the project sponsor must give the team a clear understanding of his or her expectations, allocate them appropriate resources and freedoms, offer their full support and then step back and let them get on with it. The temptation to meddle and interfere, or just to ask for regular management reports, can be potentially overwhelming for some. The project leader will have been carefully chosen and will undoubtedly keep the sponsor informed and seek guidance and support when required, especially at key stages. They are also likely to seek interaction or the presence of the sponsor and other senior leaders at key moments or events.

In turn, the project team will need to empower the informal leaders or activists in a similar way with local organizers having considerable freedom granted to them. They too must feel empowered and trusted by senior leaders. This trust, if granted freely and genuinely by senior leaders early on in the project, will be returned by project team members and employees alike, and can form a powerful foundation not just for the project at hand but for other change initiatives downstream. Building in 'change-ability' is a key by-product of the TransACT™ approach.

Placing trust in a diverse project team that has never worked together previously can seem like a huge leap for some senior leaders however I urge you to do it. Trust your people; trust your colleagues; trust the process. The results will be well worth it in the long run.

Culture by Design

Ian Adkins

Chapter 8: Structuring a Campaign

Cultural change as a campaign

So, having established the five rules for employee driven culture, we must turn our attention to how to deliver a TransACT™ project. I have tried to give some practical pointers om implementation as we have gone through the five rules so I will now focus on how to structure the project for a successful execution.

You will notice that I am increasingly switching terminology from *project* to *campaign*. That is deliberate. It is because we are creating a social movement to revolutionize an aspect of your organization; this is no ordinary project and, if your cause is powerful, will feel more like an activist campaign than routine management project.

Typically, TransACT™ is structured into four formal phases: prepare, organise, mobilise and grow. They are shown in Figure 3 as a circular and interconnected process. Any TransACT™ project or campaign will almost certainly go through this iteration a number of times. Indeed, it should cycle through as it develops, grows and becomes more effective. The first few months to a year of the project will see the first iteration of this sequence go quite deliberately through each phase.

Thereafter the campaign (project) team will run the cycle more and more quickly as the movement grows and the activist leaders develop in effectiveness.

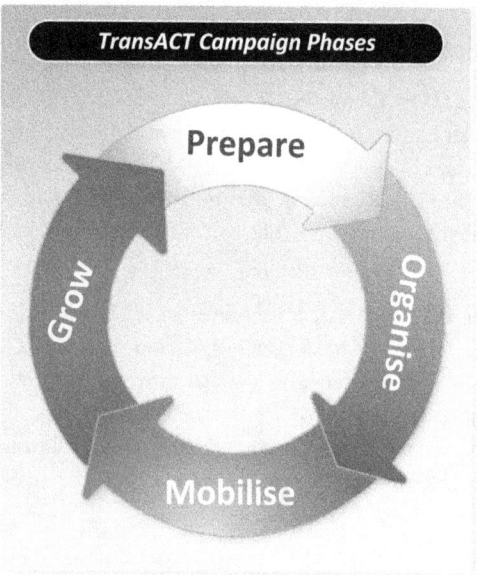

Figure 3. TransACT Phases.

A fifth element is needed on a regular basis: assessment. In-between each phase it is wise to take stock and assess progress and to learn lessons. In particular, once the movement is formed a stock-take and refocussing will be needed not just to learn lessons, but also to develop an action plan for sustaining long term organising and mobilisation activity and to refresh the organizers especially the main project team.

A timeline for culture change

A frequent, and perfectly reasonable, question at the beginning of a campaign is "how long will it all take?". Unfortunately, there are no firm guidelines and every campaign will be different and sometimes quite markedly so. You can employ TransACT™ in a company employing a few dozen people as well as a global organization employing tens or hundreds of thousands of people. The complexity of each will vary enormously as will the particular contexts and goals. Typical timelines and activities for the initial planning for a single business unit campaign based on my experience would suggest that the activities and timings in Figure 4 below, would be a reasonable start point.

Whilst these timescales can seem long compared to the siren voices of the traditional 'communicate and train' school of change managers, it is important to note that real change begins as soon as the activists come out of their activist camp and that, within weeks, changes will become noticeable in the workplace to those looking for them. Ordinary employees might be blissfully unaware of how things are changing – and that is absolutely fine. It is one of the aspects of TransACT™ that it is relatively low impact in terms of the organization as a whole. Much change will be occurring in the background whilst, behind the scenes, the campaign or

Phase	Key Activity	Timing
Prepare	The core team plan the project in outline, resource it and select a project (campaign) team drawn from across the organization.	1 – 2 months
Organise	The campaign team gathers for a launch meeting and embarks upon the detailed planning and execution of the campaign, meeting regularly and working closely as a series of work groups.	3 – 4 months
Mobilise	Mobilisation occurs once the initial wave of change activists has been selected and begin their training as well as forming up into a social movement. It builds in tempo and scale as the activists take action and the movement grows.	3 – 4 months
Grow	The growth phase is an extension of the organise and mobilise phases and sees the activists get into action and the social movement grow. It keeps going as long as required with occasional quick loops through prepare/organise/mobilise activities to keep the activist base energized, focused and well organized.	5 – 12+ months Cycling through the other phases will be required in this time too

Figure 4. Typical TransACT™ project phase timing.

Ian Adkins

project team are working tirelessly to bring everything together.

Culture by Design

Chapter 9: Campaign Team

Overview

TransACT™ can be utilized in different ways and the rules interpreted according to need and context. I could write volumes on the detail of how to put TransACT™ into practice (and may do in the future) but for now, I will offer some top-level thoughts on three key aspects of implementation that are somewhat different to many change projects. These are: the organization and composition of your campaign team; the commitment of the members of the team; and, how activists are engaged and prepared. Understanding these areas of TransACT™ will give you a sense of how to make it work in your organization and how TransACT™ implementation needs to be different from traditional change approaches.

Organization

Structuring a campaign team can be something of a personal preference and must conform to both organizational context and norms. However, TransACT™ is a different type of change and requires a different type of team and team-structure from usual change initiatives. Fundamentally the team must be predominantly composed of enthusiastic employees from across the organization. It should represent a diverse array of talents, backgrounds and experience. Jon

Culture by Design

Katzenbach identifies the leader's instinct to *"leave culture to the people professionals"*[25] but stresses that culture change is a cross-organizational effort. He cites a case study in which a huge and successful transformation was undertaken by Aetna Inc and identifies the importance of what they called *'purpose driven councils'* which were cross-functional groups which each had a clear purpose; were composed of respected people with strong informal connections; and, were given clear authority over the area they were responsible for. This is a model that I suggest is ideal for adaptation and use for our TransACT™ campaign team.

What needs to be common in the campaign team members, whatever their background, is an eagerness to be part of the change. I also suggest that the majority of the team, if not all of them, work on this on a part time basis. We need to demonstrate to the activists that this is an initiative that has been designed by people like them, not just the *'people professionals'*, and by people who really understand what life is like where they work. If we get this right, then the whole project establishes an authenticity and an integrity right from the start.

You will almost certainly want to have one or two experts drawn into your team who understand this sort of change methodology who can help to guide, support and facilitate team-working however they are there in

[25] Katzenbach. J., & Harshak, A. (2012). Stop blaming your culture. In *Don't blame your culture*. Booz & Company eBook retrieved from Amazon Kindle.

an enabling capacity not in a delivery capacity. I have worked as part of a large team of consultants many times where we took over a large corner of the client's office, planned our initiative in detail and then, with the project sponsor's blessing, took the changes out to the organization, engaging stakeholders directly and delivering the changes, whatever they were on our client's behalf. Fundamentally, this approach will not work in TransACT™. For TransACT™ to work effectively it has to be employee-led.

It is not uncommon to have a small core team (a project leader and project coordinator at a minimum) to provide all of the centralised planning, coordination, resourcing, administration and so on for the team. That might be drawn from the project sponsor's department or team and include a TransACT™ expert. However, the campaign team as a whole consists of a diverse array of talent from across the organization and the team as a whole should have considerable autonomy in how the project evolves and the decisions that are made. Think back to the SCARF model and use it to ensure that the campaign team is highly motivated from Day 1 and feels in charge of its destiny.

The campaign team will need to be structured into three broad work groups as shown in Figure 5: Campaign Architecture, Campaign Capability and Campaign Operations. In brief, these are responsible for:

▶ **Campaign Architecture.** The overall planning, coordination, resourcing, progress tracking and external connections for the whole campaign. This team looks at the big picture: it sees the campaign in context within the organization, ensures the sponsor and other senior leaders are briefed when required, secures the budget required and keeps track of all aspects of progress. It will work closely with the Campaign Leader. In short: its focus is 'up and out', and on plans, resources, coherence and key stakeholders.

▶ **Campaign Capability**. This is where the organizing magic happens with a focus on selecting, developing and supporting the activists. This team is there to design and develop a powerful engine that will drive the campaign. It works within the parameters set out by the Architecture team but, crucially, does not get involved in the day-to-day activities of the activists. That is for the Operations team. The Capability team will design and deliver the activist selection process

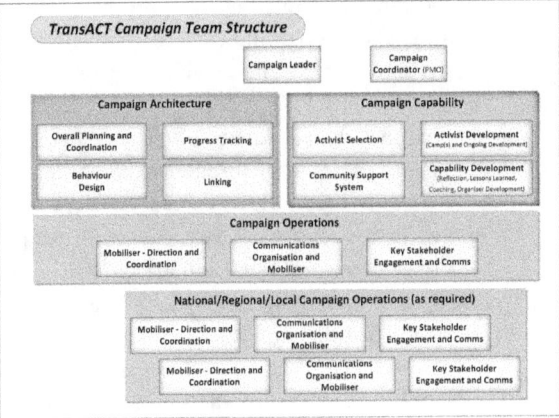

Figure 5. Campaign Team Structure.

and the activist camp(s) where activists are trained
and prepared. They will also create the digital and
analogue tools that the social movement will use
but are not responsible for the content and cura-
tion of these. Again, that is for Operations. The
Capability Team will be the primary focus up until
the activist camp(s) is delivered then it switches to
a supporting role. In short: its focus is inwards
and on creating the right human capital plus systems and tools.

▶ **Campaign Operations**. The Operations team
sit in the background in the early stages of the
project, helping the Capability team, but as soon
as the activists leave their activist camp(s) then
the Operations team takes over, helping to direct,

coordinate, energize and support the activists, turning a group of individual activists into a cohesive movement. The activities they get involved with will vary from campaign to campaign but what they do will be vital to the success of the initiative. In larger organizations, there will also need to be a cascade of operations teams to take oversight at different levels: potentially from global to regional, then national to local level. Every situation will be different. The key balancing act that they will need to perform is to focus on both the organizing and mobilising functions, supporting and energising activists, not acting as an alternate management chain. They will look for emerging activist leaders and help them to develop; share stories of successes; run events to connect activists and look for local initiatives to reinforce and to share more widely. Much of this will occur in the background to normal work and apart from occasional larger gatherings should not consume a significant amount of time. In short: its focus is down and across, on people, activities and two-way communications.

Campaign teams vary in size but typically range from 10 to 30 people depending on the size of organization and the scope of the project. The diversity of the team is key, and not just in terms of organizational departments; there should be a good mix of long serving employees, younger high potential staff and even one or two relatively new joiners. By having a diverse team, we collect together not just a broad array of talent to lead behavioural change but also the ability to embed the capability to lead this sort of change both now and for the long term. These people become a repository of knowledge and one that is spread across the organization. This is true knowledge, rather than recorded lessons learned, which is invested in people who will use the insights gained to lead further change in the future. This is something I have seen missing all too often on the projects that I have been involved with and am now a strong advocate of embedding corporate learning in this way.

It is the campaign team who will not only design and orchestrate the campaign; they will ultimately be the face of the campaign internally. We must not overwhelm people too early in case they are fearful of this role but once they have been involved for a while their energy and passion will overcome their nerves. They will be encouraged to use their creative talents too and this will help them to take ownership of the project. This is one of the aspects that your TransACT™ consultant, if you're using one, will be able to facilitate and enable.

Commitment

I would suggest from experience that most of the main team will usually work on this part-time but should expect to give a reasonable amount of time to it, perhaps one day per week over the first 4 or 5 months of the project. Their commitment and energy in shaping and leading this work will be vital if the activists are to be selected, engaged, energized and organized into an effective social movement to deliver lasting behavioural change. The selection of the team is key to its success: everyone in the team needs to be enthusiastic, keen and ready for an exciting challenge. They will need to work hard when they are on the project but will get an enormous sense of satisfaction and achievement from being involved. It will also be a good professional development opportunity especially for the more junior, high potential, members.

There will inevitably be a tension with other priorities for everyone in the campaign team and it will require the senior managers to release their people and ensure the TransACT™ campaign is given a high priority for the individuals involved and they are protected from overload or split loyalties.

Activist Camps

The centrepiece of the approach in launching real change is the activists' camp(s). These are typically planned as 2 day events which will be organized and run by the campaign team; they will generate a lot of energy and internal communications; there will be a real energy and buzz that comes from these both directly, but also indirectly as the activists talk about the events. It is important to note that the activist camps are not ends in themselves. They are the means by which we prepare and engage the activists and set them off on their journey as part of a new social movement within the business. Growing, developing and energizing this social movement will take as much, if not more, effort overall than running the activist camps but this subsequent activity is lower key and run more in the background of day to day activities – this is how real culture change takes place.

The project team will devote much time and energy to designing and delivering the activist camp(s). These are show piece events and can be quite elaborate, though this is not necessary. What is vital is that the campaign team members are front and centre for much of the event, supported where required by senior leaders and their TransACT™ consultants.

The camp(s) will become all-consuming activities as the big day approaches and there is always a tension between the need to lay on a great event and the need to focus on the building of the social movement which begins immediately after the camp(s) has concluded. This subsequent phase of activity will require significant energy and attention which is why there is a separate operations team to lead this whilst the capability development team focuses on the activist camp and the design of the activist support systems. There is in effect a transfer of lead responsibility from one team to another as the camp ends and this allows for a smooth transition and no loss of momentum.

Culture by Design

Having outlined the organization and composition of the campaign team and the initial engagement of activists it is now time to get down to next steps and for you to get into action yourself.

Ian Adkins

Chapter 10: Getting into Action

Committing to Action

Deciding that you need to change your organization and taking action are two very different things. I have spent a lot of time with clients over the years trying to help them get into action and seen how hard it can be to overcome organizational inertia. The barriers are unique to every situation but mostly come down to a fear of the unknown, which seems to drive never ending analysis in some organizations. There is frequently a need for a catalyst to force a decision to commit to action. A fear of failure drives many senior leaders and the traditionally high failure rates of culture change and the potentially nebulous nature of the benefits for many projects only reinforces this instinct.

Using the approach outlined in this book is not for the faint hearted. It requires a leadership that is willing to do something different, to trust its people, not just outside consultants or trainers, and to let go of direct control. This can seem scary and some leaders will be profoundly unsettled by this. However, they set the direction, outline the parameters, allocate resources and can have the final say in the biggest decisions. However, for this approach to work they have to let go of control of the details and to trust their people. They must also trust the process and that it will deliver tangible results.

In trying to mitigate these fears and worries, a common mistake is to try and plan the project in detail before it starts as a way of retaining leadership control. Whilst some sort of outline timeline is required, my strong advice is for the senior leaders to focus on appointing a project sponsor and a project manager, and to then let them do the rest. Crucially that will be to recruit a project team, or campaign team and then to let them plan and execute their campaign in detail. The campaign team needs to feel real ownership from the start. The principal of autonomy, of trust, needs to be established at the outset and demonstrably so. This can be hard but it's worth it in the long run.

Another question that crops up is one of resources. This is not necessarily a low budget exercise although it is likely to be much cheaper than a large consultancy-led project. The resources required though are different. You will probably still need some external support to guide, support and facilitate the process. This will most likely be a fraction of what a large consulting team would cost but you will need to account for the internal costs both in terms of time and travel costs for employees who are part of the campaign team but also for the activists once they are recruited.

The biggest single activist-related cost is likely to be the activist camp. This will vary significantly between organizations and be affected by the numbers involved, the complexity and the duration of the event. Should budgets allow, delivering this on a residential, off-site basis has to be recommended however if necessary it can also be done on a much less extravagant, in-house basis too. What is key though is that the activists physically get together as they need to talk face-to-face and have the opportunity to begin to build strong, personal connections as they will be working together over many weeks, months and years as colleagues in a cohesive social movement. The foundations of this must be built on strong bonds between the founding members of that movement. These bonds will need to be refreshed and reinforced periodically over the months to ensure those strong, human relationships are maintained.

Getting started

So, if you want to change the culture in your organization then building a coalition of support amongst the senior decision makers is crucial and getting an outline commitment to proceed is imperative so that your campaign team can begin to be formed. The whole methodology is about trust so establishing and building that from the beginning is key. Use this book as a guide, then begin to build your coalition of supporters to begin developing some momentum. Above all though focus on Rules 1 and 2. Try to define a cause which excites energy and passion, and begin to look at what behaviours you might want to change and how these might deliver the changes you would like to see. Then you can work on bringing an understanding of Rules 3, 4 and 5 to your organization so that uncertainties are reduced in the minds of decision makers and a better understanding of the start-point, the possibilities and the outcome are likely. This is all about using some of the key insights on behaviours and motivation contained in TransACT™ to get your own culture change initiative started.

TransACT™ as a catalyst for action

A great way to create movement on your ideas for culture change and to build some momentum is through a TransACT™ Behavioural Audit and Activist Demonstration (T-BAAD). You can do this yourself or ask a TransACT™ consultant to help. In essence it involves a fairly quick cultural audit over a few days within your organization to help define both your start point as well as your project aims and what sort of keystone behaviours you might want to develop[26]. You will then need to establish the impact and the results these could have, and then articulate these clearly and succinctly to senior decision makers.

You will need to communicate the benefits and explain the process to create a sense of confidence, trust and certainty. Fundamental to this is to model the tenets of activist-led, behavioural change whilst constantly building trust and understanding so that a full decision to proceed can be made in confidence. One way of doing

---

[26] If you have a TransACT™ consultant they will also deepen your understanding of the methodology during this time as well.

this is to co-opt a small group of keen colleagues to help with the T-BAAD process and let them subsequently brief the decision maker(s). Let the decision maker(s) see the magic in action! Don't over complicate this though: it can be achieved in as little as 5 – 10 days, and certainly within a few weeks at most. Remember, you are trying to get to a decision to proceed not running a full project before the project!

Activists take action

Above all, take action. Activists are only activists if they take action and if you're going to start a movement of activists then it is up to you to take action.

Good luck in your endeavour. Now, get started ... TAKE ACTION!!!

Culture by Design

Ian Adkins

Bibliography

Bain US and European Acquisition Success Study (2007).

Bloch, M., Blumberg, S., & Laartz, J. (2012, October). Delivering large scale IT projects on time, on budget, and on value. *McKinsey Quarterly* (online).

Carpenter, R. (2016). *How to Find and Engage Authentic Informal Leaders.* Retrieved from https://www.strategy-business.com/blog/How-to-Find-and-Engage-Authentic-Informal-Leaders.

Cialdini, R. B. (2011). *Influence: The psychology of persuasion.* New York, NY: Collins.

Dolan, P., Hallsworth, M., Halpern, D., King, D., & Vlaev, I. (2009). *Mindspace: Influencing behaviour through public policy.* Institute for Government (UK). Retrieved from https://www.instituteforgovernment.org.uk/sites/default/files/publications/MINDSPACE.pdf.

Gibbons, P. (2015). The Science of Successful Organizational Change, how leaders set strategy, change behaviour, and create an agile culture. USA: Pearson Education.

Han, H. (2014). *How organizations develop activists.* New York, NY: Oxford University Press.

Herrero, L. (2008). *Viral Change™: the alternative to slow, painful and unsuccessful management of change in organizations.* UK: Meeting Minds.

Herrero, L. (2011). *Homo Imitans, the art of social infection: Viral Change™ in action.* UK: Meeting Minds.

Herrero, L. (2016). *Business discovers the social movement language I hope we don't corporatize it.* Retrieved from: https://leandroherrero.com/business-discovers-the-social-movement-language-i-hope-we-dont-corporatize-it/. Main blog is at: https://leandroherrero.com/

Hughes, M. (2011, Dec 6). Do 70 per cent of all organizational change initiatives really fail? *Journal of Change Management,* 11(4), 451 – 464.

Hull, K. (2017). *Getting to the Critical Few Behaviours That Can Drive Cultural Change.* Retrieved from https://www.strategy-business.com/blog/Getting-to-the-Critical-Few-Behaviors-That-Can-Drive-Cultural-Change.

Jorgenson, H., Owen, L., & Neus, A. (2013). *Making change work.* IBM Future of Enterprise.

Katzenbach, R., & Khan, Z. (2010). *Leading outside the lines.* San Francisco, CA; A Wiley.

Katzenbach. J., & Harshak, A. (2012). Stop blaming your culture. In *Don't blame your culture.* Booz & Company eBook retrieved from Amazon Kindle.

Ian Adkins

Katzenbach, R. (2016). *10 principles of organizational culture*. Retrieved from https://www.strategy-business.com/media/file/sb82_10_Principles_of_Organizational_Culture.pdf

Laseter, T. and Cross, R. (2006). *The Craft of Connection*. Retrieved from: https://www.strategy-business.com/article/06302

Rock, D. (2009). Your brain at work: Strategies for overcoming distraction, regaining focus, and working smarter all day long. New York, NY: Harper Collins.

Rock, D. (2012). Managing with the brain in mind. In *Don't blame your culture*. Booz & Company eBook retrieved from Amazon Kindle.

Sinek, S. (2011). Start with why: How great leaders inspire everyone to take action. New York: Portfolio / Penguin.

Sinek, S. (2011). Start with why. TED talk. Retrieved from http://www.ted.com/talks/simon_sinek_how_great_leaders_inspire_action.html.

Thaler, R. H., Sunstein, C. R., & Soundview Executive Book Summaries. (2010). *Nudge: Improving decisions about health, wealth, and happiness.* Concordville, Pa.: Soundview Executive Book Summaries.

Von Post, R. (2012). Eat your peas: a recipe for culture change. In *Don't blame your culture.* Booz & Company eBook retrieved from Amazon Kindle.

Ian Adkins

About the Author

 Ian Adkins is the founder of Futures by Design and creator of TransACT™, an innovative framework for organizational culture change. Ian has been a strategy and change consultant for 13 years working with a wide variety of clients from a Swiss insurance business; a global data services business; several logistic service businesses in Dubai and UK; engineering and infrastructure organizations such as BAE Systems and Network Rail, as well as UK government departments and agencies. This work has ranged from corporate strategy development and strategic cultural change programmes to leadership development initiatives, hundreds of change workshops and designing and facilitating events, large and small.

Ian also has extensive knowledge of leading people and managing complex change in demanding environments. He served as an officer in the British Army for 16 years, deploying to the first Gulf War, Northern Ireland and Kosovo. He has held strategic and operational level policy and planning appointments in the UK MOD. He was mobilised for active duty in Pakistan in 2007, commanded a 300-strong Reservist battalion, and most recently was professional head of the Reserve component of his corps.

Culture by Design

www.ingramcontent.com/pod-product-compliance
Lightning Source LLC
Chambersburg PA
CBHW070107210526
45170CB00013B/784